D0841545

STRAIGHT TALK

GRACE B. TUBBS LIBRARY
Extension 4-H Youth Building
Ames, IA 50011-3630

Also by Robert Maidment

Robert's Rules of Disorder: A Guide to Mismanagement, 1976
Simulation Games: Design and Implementation, 1973
Criticism, Conflict, & Change, 1970

Straight Talk

A Guide To Saying More With Less

ROBERT MAIDMENT

PELICAN PUBLISHING COMPANY
GRETNA 1986

Copyright © 1983
By Robert Maidment
All rights reserved

First printing, January, 1983
Second printing, October, 1986

Library of Congress Cataloging in Publication Data

Maidment, Robert.
  Straight talk.

  1. Communication.   I. Title.
P90.M26456 1982   302.2   82-12211
ISBN 0-88289-340-8

  Modified portions of this book previously appeared in *Straight Talk: A Communication Primer*, © 1980 by National Association of Secondary School Principals, Reston, Virginia.

Manufactured in the United States of America
Published by Pelican Publishing Company, Inc.
1101 Monroe Street, Gretna, Louisiana 70053

To my Dean's List:
Lindley, B. J., Dick, and Jim

Then

Don't do as I do,
Do as I say!

Now

You might choose to do as I do,
Because I *am* what I say.

I. Because I choose to, I can learn to think straight.

II. Now that I think straight, I can learn to talk straight.

III. Once I think and talk straight, I can learn to listen straight to others.

IV. Now that I think, talk, and listen straight, I can learn to write straight for others.

V. Since I think, talk, listen, and write straight, I am straight with myself and with others.

Contents

III. Listening Straight

IV. Writing Straight

V. Being Straight

Preface

Our lives are stifled by those who seek to complicate the simple. We can learn to say more with less. This book is an effort to demystify the vast, diverse, and wondrous array of human communications. It's a distillation of both research findings and marketplace observations. Compulsive, comatose, combative, and caring relationships are analyzed.

Readers will easily recognize what is happening on these pages. Some will identify their own occasional departures from straight talk. A few might choose to modify their interactive styles.

The word "talk" includes those messages flowing around, about, within, and in spite of us. Are we aware of the nuances of message giving and receiving? And, more importantly, are we communicating past experiences or promises of future ones while ignoring the insistent present—the "what is happening" in our lives? The phrase "straight talk" connotes open, candid, direct, noncompulsive, responsive, supportive, and, whenever possible, caring relationships. Being straight is simply the sum of thinking, talking, listening, and writing straight. Being accepting, aware, approachable, and assertive. Being authentic. Being ourselves. This, then, is the essence of *Straight Talk*.

I. THINKING STRAIGHT

Because I choose to, I can learn to think straight.

Accept the Uniqueness of Others

What Is Happening

We see everything with our own unique vision. It's as if we were issued a special set of goggles at birth and view our world through them. Even when we temporarily "exchange" goggles with a special friend, that person doesn't see our world the way we see it. And vision versa. Accepting another's uniqueness is the initial step for those seeking mutual understanding and acceptance.

What I Think

   After a discussion with a colleague: "For the life of me I don't know how he can see things that way!"

What I Can Learn to Think

   "My colleagues think differently. They're neither right nor wrong—just different."

Think Positively

What Is Happening

Self-deprecating thoughts immobilize us. Since (1) our behaviors reflect our thoughts and feelings, (2) our behaviors influence the thoughts and feelings of others, and (3) we can't fake our thoughts and feelings, we might as well work on shaping positive assumptions regarding our own worth. More positive speech and actions predictably and naturally follow.

What I Think

    To myself: "I don't know what's wrong with me. I can't cope anymore. Nothing I do seems to be right."

What I Can Learn to Think

    "I'm not about to let a few disappointments get me down. I've got too much going for me. Now, where's that list of things I intend to do?"

THINKING STRAIGHT NO. 3
Touch Bases with Biases

What Is Happening

We see what we want to see. Worse, we tend to seek new information to support what we already believe to be true. My thoughts and feelings about a speaker and a situation are influenced by a complex set of preconceived notions. While I cannot consciously account for these myriad variables or totally control my reactions to them, I can (1) admit to myself that I have biases, and then (2) admit to others that I have biases. Frequent touching bases with biases doesn't guarantee objectivity. It is, however, a welcome small step toward bias-free exchanges.

What I Think

Reaction to public official during TV interview: "I never agree with his views on anything!"

What I Can Learn to Think

"I usually disagree with him, but that's no reason not to listen to what he's saying *now*."

Monitor the Moods

What Is Happening

We think and speak consistently with our moods. As we feel, therefore we are. While we cannot always alter our moods, we can become aware of how they trigger behavior. We show arrogance: "Those people are really careless. They ought to know better." Or cruelty: "That was a stupid approach! Let someone else try." Or hostility: "She must have had friends in the front office to get that promotion." Or rigidity: "My way is right!" Or whatever. The behaviors mirror the moods. And the reflections can cause infections.

What I Say

Supervisor to new employee: "Burt, it must be done my way. I've been around here a long time, and I know how everything works."

What I Can Learn to Say

"I've been doing it this way a long time, Burt, but I'm open to your ideas."

THINKING STRAIGHT NO. 5
Analyze Power Sources

What Is Happening

We are defining exercising power as exerting some positive impact upon ourselves and upon others. Thinking and having are not synonymous: (1) If you think you have power and you do, you do. (2) If you think you have power and you don't, you eventually might. (3) If you think you don't have power and you don't, you don't. (4) If you think you don't have power and you do, you soon won't. Thinking that you have power is an initial step in gaining actual power. Thinking precedes acquiring.

What I Think

"I'm powerless to change her attitude."

What I Can Learn to Think

"I've been feeling powerless in this situation. First, I will believe I can effect a positive change. Second, I will consider a plan of action. Third, if there is a reasonable expectation of success, I will carry out my plan."

THINKING STRAIGHT NO. 6
Calibrate Anger

What Is Happening

Nothing undermines clear thinking more destructively than anger. Initially, there's the "annoy ploy," which I allow to unsettle me. Unrestrained, I become entrapped in an "upset net" and concentrate on getting even. Then, as if programmed, I enter the "rage stage," where aggression prevails. Note that initially I *allow* myself to become angry. Behavior, however predictable and sequential, is controllable. Unless I want other persons or situations to control me, I'd better calibrate the emotional temperature within my comfort zone.

What I Think

Careless driver passes too close to me, forcing me to the shoulder: "How close can you get? . . . You dumb jerk! I'll fix your wagon, buddy!"

What I Can Learn to Think

"Whew! . . . How close can you get? . . . I'm lucky to be alive. Good thing I was alert!"

Check Assumptions

What Is Happening

We often make unwarranted assumptions. Suppose, for example, that someone writes what appears to be a Roman numeral nine (IX) and challenges you to add *one* line to make a six. If you assume (1) that we are dealing with Roman numerals, (2) that the required line is a straight line, or (3) that letters and numerals don't mix, then your assumptions preclude an answer. The correct "line," of course, is the letter *S* (SIX). How many erroneous assumptions did you make today?

What I Say

Group leader to trainee with arms crossed (who is thinking, "It's freezing in here. Why doesn't someone turn down the air conditioning?"): "Feeling somewhat hostile this morning, George?"

What I Can Learn to Say

"George, is something bothering you this morning?"

Plan, Then Act

What Is Happening

Many crucial communications are unnecessarily prolonged, aborted, or subverted because one person with an idea, request, or suggestion casually approaches another to seek understanding and acceptance. While approaches that are casual in demeanor might contribute to the emotional climate of an interaction, approaches that are casual in thinking predictably erode the intended message. In minutes one can write down and review key ideas or questions. Although this activity won't ensure effective communication, it will guarantee a better opportunity for mutual understanding. Remember that speech instantly evaporates. We want important ideas, requests, or suggestions to condense within the listener.

What I Think

   "I'll ask the boss next time I see him if I can attend that New York seminar."

What I Can Learn to Think

   "Let's see. The boss will have some serious reservations about my time away from the office, the effectiveness of the training, and, of course, the travel budget. I'll need to be prepared to discuss these issues. What other obstacles can I predict?"

Avoid Self-imposed Constraints

What Is Happening

As workers, we exercise more control over organizational variables than we're willing to acknowledge. Some external constraints are formidable; we can't move walls or expand budgets overnight. Most of our constraints, however, are self-imposed. Such familiar laments as "They won't let us" or "I can't do that" are usually cop-outs. "I can't," for example, is typically a mask for "I don't want to" or "I won't!" This attitude locks us into boxes.

What I Think

To myself: "We can't change our billing procedures this quickly. There will be problems. Our customers have just adjusted to what we're doing now!"

What I Can Learn to Think

"Although I have some reservations about the change, I'm willing to try it. Earlier, I had misgivings about our current procedure. But now I like it."

Stay Awake

What Is Happening

A professor dreams he is lecturing to his class. He awakes, and he *is*. Chronic somnambulism. Some fall victims, others are carriers. We overlook the stark reality that we're either growing or dying. When did you last design an action plan for self-renewal? You need one. I need one. More precisely, our families, friends, and co-workers need us to need one.

What I Think

To myself: "I've taught each summer for the last seven years and I'm sounding like a broken record."

What I Can Learn to Think

"This summer I'm taking a trip to the Orient. I need a new experience."

II. TALKING STRAIGHT

Now that I think straight, I can learn to talk straight.

TALKING STRAIGHT NO. 1
Talk Now

What Is Happening

Most of us conveniently package life into neat segments of past, present, and future. Was, is, and will be. If one accepts the notion that the present, n-o-w ("no other way"), isn't where you are, but rather *how* you are, then the past isn't where you've been—it's *how* you've been where you were. Endlessly recounting the "wheres" of one's past sends most listeners up the walls. Now is all we ever own. Use it or lose it. Talk *now*.

What I Say

To anyone who appears to be listening: "On my last business trip to ————, I ————————————."

What I Can Learn to Say

To myself: "What is happening to me *now*?"

TALKING STRAIGHT NO. 2
Avoid Minimizing

What Is Happening

Any time we're told that what is important to us isn't really important, we tend to feel worse. Our concerns are very real, and we don't appreciate anyone minimizing them for us. My problem is a part of me. Discount my problem and you shortchange me. Better to deal with me. Help me deal with my problem by dealing with me.

What I Say

Lifesaving instructor to unsuccessful qualifier: "Janice, your problem isn't really as bad as it seems. Many swimmers fail this test. Just forget it. You'll do better next time."

What I Can Learn to Say

"Janice, you're really concerned about not passing this test. Let's talk about it."

Curtail the Whys

What Is Happening

We consider ourselves adroit observers of behavior and enjoy searching for causality in the behavior of others. Cite a recent action and mentally recall *why* you did what you did. Having difficulty? Here's a legitimate "why": Why do we persist in demanding that our employees tell us why they did whatever they did? Trade rationalizations for objective realities. Trade "whys" for "whats."

What I Say

   Supervisor to employee: "Sue, why didn't you follow my instructions?"

What I Can Learn to Say

   "Sue, something went wrong just now. Can you describe what happened?"

TALKING STRAIGHT NO. 4
Be Specific

What Is Happening

The most effective way for anyone to get something is to ask for it—clearly, openly, and specifically. The listener now has three basic options: (1) to comply, (2) to provide conditionally, or (3) to deny. To avoid a denial, or to defend against the hurt a denial would cause, we often express our needs covertly. As a result, the listener is unsure of what we want and has a raft of responses available to cut us adrift.

What I Say

Employee to supervisor: "When you prepare next month's work schedule, I'd like to have some input."

What I Can Learn to Say

"I need to be on the early flexitime schedule next month so I can take advantage of the company car pool."

Eliminate Shoulds

What Is Happening

Many adults, educators in particular, have a penchant for speaking in "shoulds." This generally unsolicited paternalism seems appropriate in adult-child settings. Unfortunately, "shouldism" is preemptive because it denies the listener an opportunity to make a decision. And, as you recall from your own schoolhouse experience, it is the learner who is the one universally denied. We can replace many "shoulds" by describing the effect of the other person's behavior on us. This gives the listener both a reason and a choice.

What I Say

Teacher to pupil: "Tom, you should listen when I'm talking!"

What I Can Learn to Say

"I feel annoyed when you read while I'm talking, Tom, because I now must repeat everything."

Stop When Finished

What Is Happening

One certain way to turn off a listener is to repeat a message ad nauseam. Still, we persist in belaboring (or worse, in re-birthing) our thoughts over and over and over again. Redundancies weaken the impact of a message. How many afternoon matinees can one endure? And, like most social diseases, the malady is contagious.

What I Say

All of the above.

What I Can Learn to Say

The first sentence in the paragraph. Period.

Don't Threaten

What Is Happening

A threat is a devastating killer phrase that promises dire consequences will inexorably follow a specific action. Such words, particularly when spoken under stress, are often regretted. Threats come warped in many packages—all ultimately returnable to the sender.

What I Say

Police sergeant to rookie: "The very next time you're so much as a second late for roll call, Bradley, you and I are seeing the lieutenant!"

What I Can Learn to Say

If it's the first time, perhaps nothing. Approach the breathless recruit, make eye contact, and point to your watch. Bradley will get the message. He might even appreciate your sensitivity.

TALKING STRAIGHT NO. 8
Melt the Plastic

What Is Happening

Perfunctory talk abounds. Our messages are full of empty words. These plastic pronouncements include "Drop by if you're in the area," "Give me a call sometime," "Have a nice day," and "Keep me posted." These messages are usually indiscriminate (what we say we'd say to anyone), indefinite (what we say is not clear), and impersonal (what we say conceals our feelings). The listener is left in limbo. Do you really want me to visit next time, he wonders, or are you just being polite? These superficial statements allow us to dispatch one another indiscriminately. Deal with me directly. I dislike being dispatched.

What I Say

To new business acquaintance: "Whenever you're in town, call and we can have lunch together."

What I Can Learn to Say

"When will you be back? Let's plan now to have lunch."

Scorn Sarcasm

What Is Happening

Sarcasm is a form of verbal hostility. The speaker usually takes a holier-than-thou tone in demeaning his listener. Unfortunately, such contemptuous firing from ambush causes pain. Still more unfortunately, an innocent is often the victim. While we might not be able to lessen the frequency and intensity of these barbs among employees, we can modify our own behavior by avoiding such crooked talk.

What I Say

Manager to supervisor: "Who helped you with this report, Wesley? You couldn't have done this badly by yourself!"

What I Can Learn to Say

"Perhaps my directions weren't clear, Wesley. Later this morning I'll go over them with you."

Diminish Self-preoccupation

What Is Happening

If any malady is chronically pandemic, it is preoccupation with self. An unmistakable characteristic of those afflicted is the frequent use of "I," "me," "my," and "mine." Territorial warnings. When a librarian, for example, speaks of "my library," beware. You've encroached upon a bookkeeper, not a booklender.

What I Say

Administrator to custodian: "Ben , I'm hosting a special committee in a few hours, and this place looks crummy. Your lack of concern is making *me* look bad!"

What I Can Learn to Say

"I've been overloading you lately, Ben. We'll discuss it later today. Meanwhile, give the main hall a quick sweep and join me in the meeting room. I'll help you set up before this group arrives."

Resist Topic Jumping

What Is Happening

When a conversation becomes a bit sticky, diverting is a common ploy. Topic jumping might provide relief for the speaker, but it is often disconcerting for the listener. Not only is this tactic a diversion; it is also a deprivation. The listener is deprived of the speaker's real thoughts and feelings. Moreover, when I arbitrarily alter the topic, I might be conveying feelings of uneasiness, wariness, or lack of trust in my listener.

What I Say

Interrupting a conversation: "Oh, by the way, Sam, did you know that ————————————?"

What I Can Learn to Say

"Sam, I'm very uncomfortable discussing this issue. We really don't have enough information to decide now."

Provide Deserved Recognition

What Is Happening

Most of us like receiving some indication that our work isn't going unnoticed. When we're denied occasional work-related recognition, we justifiably feel that our efforts are unappreciated. We feel as if we were invisible. One common reaction to feeling unseen is to behave in a way that ensures some response—even if it's negative. Then, at least, we no longer feel invisible!

What I Say

Coach to player who has performed unusually well in practice: Nothing.

What I Can Learn to Say

"Jim, I'm really pleased with your work today. You appear to feel good about it, too!"

Stop Scapegoating

What Is Happening

When we know who the culprit is but censure an entire group, we're scapegoating: the group must share guilt by association with an unnamed miscreant. By resorting to the if-the-shoe-fits-wear-it routine we're acknowledging ignorance of the total situation, refusing to deal directly with conflict, or capriciously abusing an entire group.

What I Say

Sales manager to sales force: "When you people turn in your reports after my deadline, you foul up the whole system."

What I Can Learn to Say

Privately, to an individual salesperson: "Let me know as soon as possible if your report will be late. When delays are anticipated, we can rework the computer schedules."

Admit Mistakes

What Is Happening

If there were an eleventh commandment etched in stone exclusively for managerial personnel, it would be: "I don't have to be right." The amount of pain inflicted by those who are permanently right and incurably righteous is incalculable. There's no problem with the master-in-charge having clout, but he or she isn't omniscient. Self-appropriated divine rights are swiftly converted to earthly wrongs.

What I Say

Supervisor to worker: "I don't care what the operator's manual says. I'm right, and it isn't!"

What I Can Learn to Say

"I admit I made a mistake."

Deal with, Don't Talk About

What Is Happening

Delay, linger, and wait specialists are easily recognized. They are certain to talk about, over, under, around, and through most issues. The trouble is they don't deal *with* them; they suffer from "aboutism." Pontification and procrastination are, at best, unwelcome polysyllables.

What I Say

Professor to dean: "Let's table the program issue. We need more time to think about a change."

What I Can Learn to Say

"We've already agreed to a program change. Before we adjourn let's adopt an action plan for doing it."

Consider Nonverbal Messages

What Is Happening

Most messages are conveyed without words. With some effort most of us can stop talking, but we're unable to stop communicating. As we learn more about body language, perhaps we can send and receive nonverbal messages with some degree of precision. When our intent is sincere, unexpected nonverbal recognition serves as a refreshing substitute for overused verbal expressions of praise.

What I Say

Manager returning typed material to a secretary who regularly performs well: "Linda, you did your usual good job."

What I Can Learn to Say

Nothing this time. Recognition can be nonverbal. With direct eye contact, a nod, and a smile, I've already said it all.

Never Belittle

What Is Happening

In any environment characterized by a few powerful older performers and many powerless younger ones, there is a tendency for the former to exploit the powerlessness, size, age, and experiential shortcomings of the latter. While belittling allows a few to feel better, it's a guarantee that most will feel worse. Might is not always right.

What I Say

Teacher to high-school sophomore: "When you have more experience, Pam, you'll be able to see what I mean."

What I Can Learn to Say

"Pam, I can see I haven't made that very clear for you. Let me try again."

Lessen the Lies

What Is Happening

Lies—bold or weak, black or white—are all crooked. The most frequently told lies purportedly include "I gave at the office" and "Your check is in the mail." Harmless? Possibly. Crooked? Yes. We can probably deceive most easily on the phone. In face-to-face situations, however, lies seldom succeed. In all untruths the liar is subtly conditioning the listener not to trust any future statements, whether they're truthful or not. When lying is likely to erode trust, it's not worth it. When it's not likely to erode trust, it's still not worth it: you can never be certain of the difference.

What I Say

   To telephone solicitor: "I've already contributed."

What I Can Learn to Say

   "Thank you, but I'm not interested."

Exorcise Excuses

What Is Happening

Another example of crooked talk is the use of excuses. Let's admit, perhaps reluctantly, that excuses are sometimes lies in disguise: "I was so busy I didn't get around to it," "I didn't think it was very important," "I forgot," "I was awaiting an authorization to proceed." Lies. All of them. Excuses, like lies, are exercises in deception. One important distinction is that excuses are self-deceiving, because lies to ourselves are easily believed. Our excuses, then, become self-fulfilling constraints as we live out the lies.

What I Say

To a colleague: "Look, I just fire the missiles around here. Where they land is *your* department."

What I Can Learn to Say

"We have a joint responsibility for this. Let's agree on what's to be done, by whom, and when, before everything blows up around here."

Avoid Verbal Abuse

What Is Happening

Whenever we load our language with abusive words, we cause our listener to become defensive. The loaded words are heard while the intended message is ignored. All abusive phrasing is noncaring: The speaker doesn't give a hoot and his words serve as livid proof. The speaker also reveals an inability to use language effectively. It's a losing situation for both speaker and listener.

What I Say

Coach to player: "What in the world is wrong with you, Gary? That's the dumbest thing you've done this afternoon!"

What I Can Learn to Say

"Gary, let's take a look at your assignment on that last play."

Take the Initiative

What Is Happening

Many interpersonal conflicts continue unresolved because one person is waiting for the other to restart the dialogue. Talking together is of course no guarantee of problem resolution, but it does assure us an opportunity to resolve our differences. I will assume you are waiting for me to contact you, so I will. Let's keep the conversation going!

What I Say

Social worker to colleague: "I'll be darned if I'll contact her again about her son. After that last conversation, oceans can freeze before I go through another hassle with her!"

What I Can Learn to Say

"However distressing our last conversation was, I will contact her today. I guess we're both trying to help her son in our own ways."

Talk Directly

What Is Happening

Much of our talk is indirect. It has something to do with prepositions. We talk "about," "despite," "around," and "through" people with varying degrees of ineffectiveness. The needed preposition here is "to." Talk *to* people. In groups notice how one will talk "about" rather than "to" another person even when that person is present. Indirect comments invite indirect responses. When you talk *to* people, they tend to respond directly.

What I Say

Supervisor in staff meeting at which Dave is present: "I'd like to hear what Dave thinks about this issue."

What I Can Learn to Say

"Dave, what is your position on this?"

Consider Not Talking

What Is Happening

In group encounters we often feel an urgency to bolster the banter. But we are not compelled to contribute, question, repeat, or yield to any other expected behavior. Group conversations can be stimulating or stifling with or without our brilliance: we need not talk compulsively. Nor need we suffer guilt from elected silence. Mercifully, some conversations might be shortened. We could then return to work. Note that we "contributed" after all!

What I Say

In conversations with colleagues: "Now, as I view it, _____."

What I Can Learn to Say

Nothing.

Guard Against Sandbagging

What Is Happening

One insidious form of sandbagging is the deliberate withholding of information, while another is speaking, which enables the informed person to look good and/or the uninformed one to look bad. It's one-upmanship at its low-downest. Embarrassment and anger predictably surface when the speaker realizes that what he has said is either inaccurate or incomplete. Whenever you're the victim of sandbagging, someone else looks good at your expense. If it happens *twice*, the sandbag becomes a door-mat. You.

What I Say

After waiting for the speaker to finish a committee report: "Doug, if you had read the new policy, you'd have known that your suggestion isn't feasible."

What I Can Learn to Say

Interrupting speaker: "Hold it a second, Doug. Did your committee have an opportunity to review the new policy?"

Shun Preaching

What Is Happening

Championing causes is an American tradition. There are, of course, many defensible stands seeking adherents. Our organizations burgeon with both champions and causes. Although the personal advocacy of economic, social, religious, or political causes on company time is tempting, it is clearly a risky venture. A safer approach is to avoid inappropriate preaching about causes while seeking insightful solutions to organizational concerns.

What I Say

City manager to council: "The proposed local refinery will be environmentally destructive, will ultimately depress waterfront property values, and will deter the growth of our seafood industry."

What I Can Learn to Say

"There might be situations when national interests could or should prevail over environmental concerns. Let's identify and discuss those apparently conflicting situations."

Eliminate Rumors

What Is Happening

Perhaps no human trait is as corrosive in organizations as the deliberate spreading of rumors, innuendos, half-truths, or truthful but very personal data. The dearth of valid, relevant, and objective information contributes to a neurotic climate. Before we add to the spread of mis-information we can ask ourselves: "Is it true?" "Will the sharing of this information benefit someone?" If the answer to either or both is negative or unknown, we can remain silent.

What I Say

    Intern to nurse: "I've heard that our administrator is dating the new psychiatrist."

What I Can Learn to Say

    Nothing.

Avoid Preempting

What Is Happening

The admonition "Stop putting words in my mouth" is a plea against preemptive behavior. While all conversations are manipulative, they don't have to be controlling. Preemptive speech is self-serving, and, like some other examples of crooked talk, it represents a denial of the other person. Preemption is particularly noticeable in conversation when the communicator "accepts" for the receiver. I don't need you to tell me what you want me to say.

What I Say

Executive to middle manager: "Dan, that sharp new regional supervisor we brought in really likes your management style. What do you think about her so far?"

What I Can Learn to Say

"What is your assessment of the new regional supervisor's work to date?"

Disdain Labels

What Is Happening

Objectivity is an important trait for anyone to develop. But we seem to have a pervasive (or "perversive") tendency to label others. We harbor overt—and covert—opinions regarding other people's intelligence, energy level, and other characteristics. Blended subjectively, these "facts" become labels. And, like fingerprints, the labels become permanent identifiers.

What I Say

Camp counselor to peer: "Jimmy is an immature, dull, and listless kid who showed no interest in anything we did last year. Besides, his parents couldn't care less about him. Hope you have better luck with him. You'll need it."

What I Can Learn to Say

"I couldn't reach Jimmy last year. I'm hopeful you'll do better."

Stress Clarity

What Is Happening

Intentionally or not, we sometimes use "insiders'" words which confuse nonmembers of our particular work or social group. Although these words and phrases might sound convincing, they illuminate little. Let's now admit that often we don't even understand each other. Of course, we might not be prepared for the consequences if we did. Straight talk would allow *everyone* to understand us. Horrors!

What I Say

School-board member to parent: "Our multigraded, individualized learning program is based upon a modified open-school approach."

What I Can Learn to Say

"Mrs. Turner, we're proposing some policy changes, and we need your ideas. Could you meet with us next Thursday?"

Make Statements

What Is Happening

Another example of indirect talk is the tendency to ask questions when we really want to make statements. The questioner clouds ownership of the idea, thus avoiding possible rejection. Notice these end-run statements at your next work or civic gathering. We can raise our assertiveness quotient a few notches by making statements undisguised as questions. Will the *real* statement please rise?

What I Say

Personnel director to boss: "Do you think it would be a good idea if I became more involved in planning our training programs?"

What I Can Learn to Say

"I want to be actively involved in planning our supervisory training programs."

Answer Questions with Statements

What Is Happening

Questions deserve answers. Frequently, however, questions elicit questions. When a person seeks information we might or should know but don't, we quickly convert our defensiveness to annoyance and respond with, "How do you expect me to know that?" The questioner is now unfairly transformed into culprit *and* victim. When we answer a question with another question, we often avoid straight talk. Ask me "know" questions, and I'll tell you no "whys."

What I Say

Regional manager to salesman asking for quarterly forecasts: "Why do you want them now? Can't you wait?"

What I Can Learn to Say

"I don't have the figures right now. I'll get them to you tomorrow."

Use Humor Constructively

What Is Happening

An elementary principal was described as "having the happy faculty of keeping a faculty happy." We know that laughter does not necessarily influence either motivation or performance. We're not talking about humor per se but about how humor is used. If one-liners are used to gloss over, to deflect, or to retreat from personal interaction, we're avoiding constructive confrontation. Remember, principals never grow old. They just lose their faculties.

What I Say

Manager to foreman: "Mike, your handling of that situation reminds me of the guy who was asked the difference between ignorance and apathy. He said he didn't know and didn't care!"

What I Can Learn to Say

"As soon as we can sit down together for a few minutes, Mike, I want to discuss that incident with you."

Unmix Messages

What Is Happening

Another curious, confusing, yet common example of crooked talk is the "yes, but" routine. The speaker provides a supportive "yes" and immediately adds a subversive "but." In a single, uninterrupted sentence one hears: "That was a fine report, but there are still many issues you didn't address." Here, a compliment is followed by censure. Which message does the listener receive? Part two. We seek opportunities for improvement in our work. And we need recognition. We don't, however, want these messages mixed. Plaudits and audits require separate packaging.

What I Say

Boss to secretary: "Your typing skills have really improved recently, Anne, but you obviously didn't proof these letters."

What I Can Learn to Say

"Anne, your typing really has improved recently! After you proof these letters carefully, I'll sign them."

Keep Cool

What Is Happening

We're involved daily in hundreds of interpersonal contacts. To expect that all of these interactions will be cordial and productive is naive. We can all recall, for example, when we felt that one more complaining client, one more antagonistic colleague, or one more interruptive call would ignite an explosion. Muttering "Cool it!" to ourselves only delays the outburst. We need to face crisis situations rationally. Less stress means less mess.

What I Say

Male coach to female coach: "You know what you can do with Title IX. I want the court an additional thirty minutes today! Don't you people realize my season opens on Friday?"

What I Can Learn to Say

"Shirley, I need some additional court time tomorrow. Can we discuss it later over coffee?"

TALKING STRAIGHT NO. 35
Perceive Others Positively

What Is Happening

Another example of self-sabotage is our tendency toward immobilizing perceptions of others. It's called the SCRUB approach to human interaction: we literally "scrub out" those we perceive as Sick, Clumsy, Rowdy, Ugly, or Bad. Overreacting by substituting pleasant illusions for what we perceive as ugly realities is another means of avoiding a productive exchange. An OPEN approach—Objective, Participative, Exploring, and Noncompulsive—is more promising. These attitudes, when reflected in our actual behavior, signal a willingness to care in any given interaction. They can help turn pleasant illusions and ugly realities into pleasant realities.

What I Say

Nurse to co-worker: "Did you ever have to deal with such a (sick, clumsy, rowdy, ugly, bad) patient?"

What I Can Learn to Say

"That patient deserves all of the professional care and attention I can possibly provide. Until now, our contacts have been unproductive. They *will* improve. Starting now. Starting with me."

Retire the War Stories

What Is Happening

War stories are personal accounts, usually exaggerated, which somehow survive from other times and other places, only to be reincarnated under less than optimal circumstances. War stories tend to lionize the teller. They also tend to be completely irrelevant. The speaker is really saying, "My exploits deserve a hearing, and you're elected to hear them." The listener, in turn, fidgets, fakes attention, and finds new ways to avoid future encounters with this warrior.

What I Say

To colleague as meeting adjourns: "Say, our discussions today remind me of that time in ——————, when I met ——————————, and we —————————, and then I —————————— . . ."

What I Can Learn to Say

"What are some implications of our decisions today?"

Don't Play Therapist

What Is Happening

We've all studied a little psychology. And a little knowledge can be a dangerous thing. Recognizing deviance is a legitimate aspect of a manager's role. Treating deviance clearly is not. Make referrals to designated counselors, psychologists, and others who are trained and licensed in their specialties. You can then work with individuals consistently with the professional advice. This practice is both ethical and sensible.

What I Say

Manager to subordinate: "You probably have a personality disorder. Now, if I were you, I'd ——————————————————."

What I Can Learn to Say

"You've had some very stressful situations here recently. Would you consider talking with the employee relations counselor?"

Create Confidence

What Is Happening

Do you recall having your confidence crushed by an authority figure? Those who unwittingly erode our confidence extract an incalculable toll in human resources. The formula for failure is familiar: issue vague instructions, frequently modify directions, set unrealistic deadlines, fail to define expectations, assign tasks beyond a reasonable level of competence, or show disdain for those seeking clarification. The top award for insensitivity goes to the person who wants every task performed precisely his or her way. End of confidence. End of creativity. End of caring.

What I Say

Boss to secretary: "Karen, why can't you ever get these reports finished on time? I wanted this one yesterday, didn't I?"

What I Can Learn to Say

"Let's reexamine your work load, Karen. Perhaps I've been expecting you to do more than you can handle alone."

Talk Sparingly

What Is Happening

Most of us talk too much. An excellent example of this phenomenon is the typical college classroom, where the law of two-thirds prevails. Two-thirds of the time someone is talking. Two-thirds of the time that someone is the instructor. And two-thirds of what the instructor says is irrelevant. Quite an indictment! Save the words for information which can't be packaged more appropriately—for giving directions, motivating, and (on occasion) evaluating. Tellers are for banks.

What I Say

Instructor to class: "Let me review for you
(a) the political conditions leading to the War of 1812"
(b) what Melville really meant"
(c) the Laffer Curve"

What I Can Learn to Say

Nothing now. Select another method. It will be better; you can bet on it.

Avoid Giving Advice

What Is Happening

Perhaps nothing preempts a listener more thoroughly than gratuitous advice. Ironically, when people appear to be seeking advice, they usually don't want it; they're more likely to be looking for an active listener. The person receiving advice always determines the relevance and quality of counsel. If I follow your advice, it is only because I am willing to, and because my advice to myself just happens to coincide with your advice to me. I'd rather you just help me advise myself. And keep your advice to yourself.

What I Say

Manager to supervisor: "If you'd take my advice, you'd take the afternoon off."

What I Can Learn to Say

"Kevin, you seem very upset about what happened. Perhaps you'd like to talk about it."

Validate the Visual

What Is Happening

We reveal much of our uniqueness through the language of the body. Gestures and posture sometimes tell far more than words. But whether we can monitor these natural messages correctly is questionable. Reading body language is an inexact art; we can't unerringly and consistently perceive other peoples' emotional states by observing their demeanor. Crossed arms, for example, can project defiance, rejection, self-satisfaction, isolation, hostility, or authority. The body does provide cues for the attentive listener, clues to the speaker's feeling, and hues of ever-changing human moods as speaker and listener interact. Notice what is happening, but evaluate what you see carefully.

What I Say

To myself: "She's avoiding eye contact and covering her mouth with her hands. She's obviously lying."

What I Can Learn to Say

"She seems unsure. I'll check it out with her so I will know what she really wants to say to me."

Own Your Feelings

What Is Happening

There isn't very much we really own. But what we do own is vital. We own the interval between birth and death. And we own our own feelings. When I'm angry, it's because I choose to be angry at that moment. If I blame you for my being angry, then I no longer own my anger. My feelings in any situation are uniquely mine. Since I can't give them to anyone else, why try? Better to deal with my own feelings, acknowledge them, and, most importantly, be accountable for them.

What I Say

Parent to son: "You're making me angry, Jeff! Keep doing that and you'll *never* see those car keys again."

What I Can Learn to Say

"Jeff, I'm annoyed when you return the car with an empty tank because I worry about running out of gas before reaching the station."

Continue Refining Skills

What Is Happening

Improving communication skills is a lifetime pursuit. But sometimes practice makes imperfect; verbal imperfections can be repeated until they become habits. We have learned unproductive speaking skills, and we can also unlearn them—that is, if we want to. If we don't want to, perhaps we should vacate those places where interpersonal skills are needed. Permanently.

What I Say

To anyone who will listen: "Don't expect me to change. That's the way I am. Nothing in my job description says I have to like what I do or the people I work with!"

What I Can Learn to Say

Either: "I'm planning to attend a communications workshop. Any recommendations?" Or: "I'm quitting."

Choose Your Space

What Is Happening

Life is a many-splintered thing. When all that we're guaranteed is the insistent presence called "now," our personal decisions regarding time, energy, and talent are vital. A commitment to anything requires an investment of these resources. Because we're unable to commit to everything, we need to choose our space. When we voluntarily and selectively invest our personal resources in meaningful activities, we're more likely to be happy and productive. What I want to do is what I would do even if I didn't have to.

What I Say

Secretary to boss: "I'll cancel my plans and come in on Saturday."

What I Can Learn to Say

"Sorry, I've made personal plans for the weekend."

III. LISTENING STRAIGHT

Once I think and talk straight, I can learn to listen straight to others.

LISTENING STRAIGHT NO. 1
Listen by Observing

What Is Happening

Most of us hear ably, but listen ineptly. Did you ever wonder why we can find numerous courses on public speaking but precious few on public listening? We can teach ourselves to be better listeners by becoming better observers. Because most messages are delivered visually, we listen largely with our eyes. So if I'm not really seeing you, I'm not really listening to you either. Fortunately, observation is a skill we can develop. Continuously.

What I Say

To myself: "Since the telephone is the next best thing to being there, I'll call."

What I Can Learn to Say

When talking on the phone: "Say, when I can't see you, I can't hear you. Drop by and let's really talk it over."

Listen Attentively

What Is Happening

Unless I consciously determine to listen to another person, I'm not going to receive the message. Hearing is a science; listening is an art. When I fail to listen to you attentively, I miss more than your specific message: I could miss portions of our next conversation, because I've already revealed my lack of interest in your message and/or my lack of concern for you. Unless I can accept the cumulative consequences of my inattentiveness, I'd better listen to you now.

What I Say

To myself: "I thought I heard what he said. I guess I just wasn't listening."

What I Can Learn to Say

"Next time I'm going to repeat his instructions in my own words so that there will be no misunderstanding."

LISTENING STRAIGHT NO. 3
Listen Smart

What Is Happening

While our brains race, our talk crawls. Those milliseconds between words and sentences permit us to tune out the speaker's voice and tune in our own. Just as a speaker can't improve a message by talking faster, the listener can't improve on message reception by thinking more slowly. The listener can, however, use these precious moments between words and ideas to anticipate, to review, and to analyze. Wandering during a conversation leaves us wondering after it.

What I Say

To myself: "I wonder what he said. Well, it couldn't have been important!"

What I Can Learn to Say

Again, to myself: "He wouldn't be taking my time to discuss this without good reason. Let's see if I can summarize his comments."

LISTENING STRAIGHT NO. 4

Listen If You Don't Want To, But Have To

What Is Happening

When you're talking, I have a choice: I can passively watch or actively listen. If I perceive your message to be uninteresting, I become a watcher. If I try to fake interest, my energies are concentrated on the faking. It's counterproductive to practice faking interest, because as my acting skill increases I'll use it more often and I'll hear even less. I might as well use the same energy to force myself to listen. It's a matter of practice. When I work on developing genuine interest and on actively listening to you, it's a winning situation for both of us. Not only might I learn something, but the likelihood is that you'll be more attentive to me the next time I have a message for you.

What I Do

While listening to a colleague I fake interest and allow my mind to wander.

What I Can Learn to Say and Do

"Leslie, I want to summarize the three points you made before we talk further."

LISTENING STRAIGHT NO. 5

Don't Listen If You Don't Want To and Don't Have To

What Is Happening

There is no payoff in enduring any conversation that is of no benefit if you don't have to. As we've noted, listening requires energy, time, and talent. Treat unwelcome office interlopers and telephone interruptors to straight talk. Tell them clearly, politely, and directly that higher priorities must prevail.

What I Say

To myself: "It would be unkind to say that I don't feel like listening to him now."

What I Can Learn to Say

To him: "Could we continue this conversation later? I don't feel as though I can give you my full attention now."

LISTENING STRAIGHT No. 6
Evaluate the Emotion

What Is Happening

Messages transmit both thoughts and feelings. When a disparity exists between the thought and the feeling, we tend to trust the latter. If a speaker enthuses about something that also energizes me, I can be enticed by the energy and miss the message. Such overstimulation can be countered objectively. After mentally ignoring the speaker's enthusiasm, I can think: "What is being said?"; "How is this message affecting me?"; and "Do I really want to share in the speaker's enthusiasm?" Whenever I'm verbally seduced, I am at once both victim and culprit.

What I Hear

Local TV commercial: "Come see us this weekend for the biggest deal on the biggest seller by the biggest car dealer . . ."

What I Can Learn to Say

To myself: ". . . telling what may be the biggest lie I've heard today. I want a new car, but what are the facts about this deal?"

Accept Sincere Compliments

What Is Happening

Often we deflect well-intended and deserved praise with, "Oh, it was nothing. Anyone could have done as well." Or "It's just part of my job." Such deft deflections by the listener could provide the speaker with one of two messages: (1) "You really don't know what you're talking about" or (2) "I don't deserve to hear what you're saying." A more positive reaction to the initial compliment would be to accept and to savor.

What I Hear

Boss to secretary: "Jean, that was a splendid piece of work you did on the annual report."

What I Can Learn to Say

"Thank you."

Accept Caustic Comments

What Is Happening

The law of the equivalent zap suggests that sooner or later revenge will be ours. The temptation to render comeuppance to the zapper often seems irresistible. However inviting it might be for us to destroy the zapper, the best defense is *not* offense. The best defense is to accept and to ignore. This behavior defuses the zapper.

What I Hear

Physician to associate: "Hey, Harry, I really like your new jacket! Too bad they didn't have your size."

What I Can Learn to Say

"Thanks, Dick, I'm glad you like it."

LISTENING STRAIGHT NO. 9
Accept Irrelevant Compliments

What Is Happening

In work settings we occasionally receive compliments that are not job-related and are, therefore, usually irrelevant. Favorable notice by a supervisor of a new article of clothing, for example, might make you wonder, "What did he think about how I looked yesterday, when he didn't say anything?" Again, an appropriate response is to acknowledge and to ignore. Favorable comments that are job-related seldom cause the listener to wonder about the speaker's intent.

What I Hear

Supervisor to employee: "Susan, I really like that outfit you're wearing today."

What I Can Learn to Say

"Thank you."

Avoid Stressors

What Is Happening

We inexorably collect our share of stresses from most events in life. Of course, people as well as events can cause stress. Such people are called "stressors"; they're the carriers who don't *have* ulcers, but *give* them. While many of these stress inducers can't be avoided, a few emphatically can. If you don't live with or work for a stressor, you can skillfully evade, ignore, or escape them. With stress it's not how you win the race, but how you trim the pace.

What I Hear

A compulsive friend: "C'mon Bob, hurry it up! Grab your coat and let's go! If we don't run, we'll miss the pregame warm-ups. Let's go!"

What I Can Learn to Say

"Go on ahead. I'll see you at the game."

Allay Annoyances

What Is Happening

One cause of ineffective listening is allowing ourselves to be distracted by the speaker's annoying behavior. When I mentally count the "you know"s someone tacks on sentence endings I'm obviously not listening. Aggravating as the habit may be, I need not permit another to control me. What to do? Well, if a close colleague has profoundly bad breath, I can (1) ignore and suffer, (2) proffer a breath freshener, (3) sneak mouthwash to the offender's desk, or (4) confront in a straight, open, and constructive manner. Four options. But only one choice is straight.

What I Hear

Business associate popping gum when he talks: "Click . . . click . . . click . . . click . . . et clickera . . ."

What I Can Learn to Say

"Charley, when you pop your gum like that, I become distracted and can't concentrate on what you're saying."

Minimize Distractions

What Is Happening

Many factors distort our communications. Attitudes, feelings, and personality are among those factors that filter and alter messages. There are environmental factors that also distort messages. Work stress, time limitations, and interruptions are among the environmental distractions we face. While we exercise little control over the attitudes, feelings, and personality of our listener, we can usually minimize those outside influences. Assuring privacy, reducing interruptions, and selecting neutral or nonwork sites for important discussions are more than simply comfort considerations. Less distraction means less distortion. More focus, less fracas.

What I Hear

Manager to colleague: "This is probably as good a time and place as any to discuss our differences."

What I Can Learn to Say

Colleague: "We're both exhausted, and we can't guarantee privacy here. Our concerns deserve a better setting. Don't you agree?"

IV. WRITING STRAIGHT

Now that I think, talk, and listen straight, I can learn to write straight for others.

Provide Incentives

What Is Happening

A quiet room, a flat writing surface, and a blank tablet. Ready to write? Wrong. The head is also quiet, flat, and blank. To see the light, increase the heat. Incentives. We can exploit the relationship between the effort required and the reward anticipated. While neither might be substantially altered, we can explore some options. By writing in small doses and systematically rewarding tangible efforts, we can complete the necessary task. After writing a page or two we can take a walk, a drink, or a nap. The important word is *after*. See the light? Now write!

What I Do

Manager starting to write a report: "Hmmmmm . . . wonder how I should begin this . . . It's probably going to take a long time to finish . . . Hmmm . . ."

What I Can Learn to Do

"I can outline this report and write the introduction within an hour. I'll call Fred now. Maybe we can play racquetball during lunch."

WRITING STRAIGHT NO. 2
Express, Don't Impress

What Is Happening

A college English instructor provided me with a lifetime lesson in clarity. On a failing theme he scrawled, "The prolixity of your verbosity is abominable!" Those seven words, imprinted forever within my brainpan, have since cautioned me to express rather than impress. Why, after all, extol the virtues of salubrity, opulence, and sagacity when we'd much prefer being healthy, wealthy, and wise? Besides, those heavy words are harder to spell.

What I Write

The prolixity of your verbosity is abominable!

What I Can Learn to Write

Keep it simple.

Tighten the Prose

What Is Happening

If we wrote as we spoke, most of us would communicate more effectively. We inexplicably tend to load our written language with excess verbiage. Unconscious obfuscation. This verbal overkill literally deadens messages. One panacea is to use fewer esoteric words like "panacea" or "esoteric." Another cure is to use fewer words in shorter sentences. Say it. Stop it. Scan it. Sign it. Stuff it. Seal it. Stamp it. Send it.

What I Write

Due to the fact that I never received my previous order I'm now reordering the merchandise in the same fashion as before.

What I Can Learn to Write

I haven't received my order. Please check it.

Say It, Don't Write It

What Is Happening

Vocal inflections provide shades of meaning. How we say something is often more important than what we say. In writing, however, these helpful inflections are absent and misinterpretation is a frequent result. Take the sentence "We didn't say you should retire." When the *We* is emphasized, our message suggests that someone else made the statement. The *didn't*, emphatically voiced, expresses outright denial. We didn't *say* it may imply that we recommended it in an executive memo. And, Jim, we didn't mean *you*; we meant a manager in another section. Further, we didn't say you *should*—we were suggesting only that you *consider* retiring. Finally, we didn't say you should *retire*. We were suggesting a leave of absence. Some things are better said than read.

What I Write

In a memo: We didn't say you should retire.

What I Can Learn to Write

On a memo pad: Call Jim for lunch.

Commit to Print

What Is Happening

We've encouraged face-to-face interactions as a way to reduce interpersonal conflict. Certainly a willingness to converse increases the *opportunity* for diminishing dissonance. But if we want a *guarantee* that an accurate record of what was said will be available later, we rely upon a familiar dictum: Put it in writing. There are two important cautions to observe, however, *before* we commit to print: (1) Write *when* a record is required, then (2) write only *what* is required. Consider the potential reduction in our monumental paper overburden if these cautions were observed. Make the paper chase a proper choice.

What I Write

Anything, all the time.

What I Can Learn to Write

What's necessary, when necessary.

Know Your Target

What Is Happening

Advertisers extol to control. Mystery writers weave to deceive. Journalists perform to inform. Evangelists aspire to inspire. Revolutionaries write to incite. Most of us, however, string words together on paper only on demand. When written messages are appropriate, we can learn from those who prevail with the pen. They've mastered a most basic lesson: They know their audience and carefully aim their words at their intended target. A few key questions can focus our writing: Who is going to read what we write? What are they like? What do they already know? What do they need to know? What do I want them to know? What do I want them to do after they know what I want them to know?

What I Think

Manager starting a report: "Let's see, I'll apply the usual who, what, when, where, and why routine to this material."

What I Can Learn to Think

"Let's see. First, who's going to *read* this?"

Write Right

What Is Happening

Impreciseness in speech is occasionally tolerated. At least it is immediately correctable. Not many hackles are raised by an "It's me" or an "irregardless" or two. Put it in writing, however, and the consequences can be calamitous. A missing word, a mangled phrase, or a misplaced sentence can severely alter the meaning of one's message. Although one can write incorrectly and still send readable messages, it helps to be both clear and correct. Written misstatements are difficult to retract.

What I Think About My Writing

Eliminating dangling participles and avoiding misspellings results in gooder grammer.

What I Can Do About My Writing

Use an editor's guide or a guiding editor.

Stop Unintended Messages

What Is Happening

While we can't control a reader's reaction to our writing, we can improve readability by removing unintentional messages. The newspaper headline SCHOOL BOARD BANS SEX BEHIND CLOSED DOORS serves as a classic reminder to check our messages carefully. When we cause readers to guess what we meant to write, we invite misunderstandings. Open doors and clarity soars.

What I Write

The school board banned sex behind closed doors.

What I Can Learn to Write

While in executive session, the school board developed a new policy on sex education.

Trim the Hedges

What Is Happening

We frequently use memos or letters to disguise our real message. We employ written masquerades because they are less disquieting than face-to-face encounters; writing also allows us to conceal facts and feelings. This tactic is known as hedging. If, for example, you "hedge" in a written statement, the message you actually convey might be one of dislike, indecisiveness, avoidance, or lack of trust. Why beat around the bush when you can trim the hedges and increase understanding?

What I Write

Memo from manager to supervisor: If feasible, we might consider your request later when it might be more appropriate.

What I Can Learn to Write

Your request cannot be granted now. Please drop by this week to discuss other options.

Seek Help

What Is Happening

Want a guarantee from this section? Want to be absolutely certain that your office correspondence can face mail even when it's not fail-safe? Share letters and memos with a similarly determined colleague. Expurgate polluting in the proof. An associate once noted that I used the word "frequently" thirteen times in three pages. That's now something I don't often do. Just as talented editors underscore the oversights, colleagues can proof letters or carbons periodically to make certain that our messages are clear, concise, and correct. It works. Guaranteed! Incidentally, should you want additional practice, the editors left four errors in this book for you to uncover.

What I Say

Middle manager to himself: "I wish I could be certain that these memos are clear. Well, once they're distributed, I'll find out soon enough!"

What I Can Learn to Say

"Before I distribute these memos, I'll ask one of the supervisors to read them."

Write Something

What Is Happening

For most of us writing is a formidable task. It is even more difficult when our jobs require us to write about uninteresting topics. When we're facing the pressure of arbitrary deadlines, our ability to produce often diminishes. The key to this dilemma, of course, is to sit down and write. Right now. Writing something is better than writing nothing. Later editing might convert the something from worthless to worthwhile. Most writers experience these initial blocks. Page blight is to authors as stage fright is to actors.

What I Once Wrote

You can't extract something from nothing.

What I Now Write

I once was a pessimist.

V. BEING STRAIGHT

Since I think, talk, listen, and write straight, I am straight with myself and with others.

BEING STRAIGHT NO. 1
Keep Stretching

What Is Happening

One particularly insidious self-constraint is the lament "I'm too old for that!" Of course, we can substitute "intelligent," "mature," or another word for "old." These self-applied adhesives literally stick us in place. But since growth is never static, our skills either stretch or shrink. Look around you. Do you perceive a friend or colleague to be torpid at twenty? Or frozen at forty? Or senile at sixty? Self-imposed barriers are often the most difficult to overcome. Who ever said growing was painless?

What I Think

"I'm beyond the point where any athletic involvement would be helpful."

What I Can Learn to Think

"There's no reason I can't start a physical conditioning program. I'm checking with my doctor tomorrow."

Take Charge

What Is Happening

We consistently make decisions affecting our personal wellness. Such decision making is an undeniable right. Once we choose to exercise this right, we assume the responsibility for doing it. We also have the capacity for change. But having the *willingness* to take charge of our lives is the crucial factor. Having the right, the responsibility, and the capacity is worthless without the willingness. I'm the one who must decide to get off a path leading nowhere. I get off by *doing* it. It's not the I.Q. or the "I could"; it's the "I will."

What I Say

"I want to make some major changes in my life."

What I Can Learn to Say

"I want to make some major changes in my life . . . and I *will*!"

Continue the Conversation

What Is Happening

Although temporariness is pervasive, an interrupted relationship is not necessarily terminated. Conversations continue as we review previous dialogues and rehearse future ones. Since realities aren't destinies, our parting—amicable or otherwise—is simply an abrupt cessation of something called "now." "Good-bye" is more precisely "Good-bye for now." The poetic "Till we meet again" captures the essence of continuing contact. As long as one of us remains "talking," the conversation continues.

What I Say

To myself, about a faraway friend: "Out of sight, out of mind."

What I Can Learn to Say

"Out of sight, temporarily; out of mind, never."

Strive to Care

What Is Happening

Throughout these pages we have stressed many basic notions about communication, stretched some, and speculated upon others. One cohesive thread is apparent. Straightjacket thinking, speaking, listening, and writing are anathema to being straight. We cannot nurture open, exploring, supportive, and responsive relationships with self-sabotaging, immobilizing behaviors. No relationship is fail-safe, but if my style of communicating with you is compulsive, combative, or comatose our relationship is sure to fail. If it's caring, we have a chance. And an opportunity.

What I Think

Regarding a troublesome colleague: "We can never work together harmoniously. That's just the way things are."

What I Can Learn to Think

"I want and need a better relationship. I'll start by being straight with him."

Be Straight

What Is Happening

We'll end this conversation with a fifteen-word summary: "Be straight, play fair, tell the truth, keep your word, and avoid insensitivity to others." Whatever the interaction, we're far safer and saner when we do things *with* others. Not to them. Not for them. Not despite them. Not beyond them. But with them. Imagine what it would be like if straight talk became standard talk in all human interactions. If we continue to refine our communication skills, ultimately our messages will be received perfectly. Well . . . almost perfectly.

What I Say

"Practice makes perfect."

What I Can Learn to Say

"Perfect practice makes perfect."